# Puerto Rican
# Vegan Cookbook

Jacinia Perez

Minimalist Vegan Lifestyle

This book is licensed for your personal kitchen journey. This book is the result of months in the kitchen to get each dish just right. If you would like to share this book with another person, please purchase an additional copy for each recipient whenever possible. If you're reading this book and did not purchase it, I would hope that you will think of purchasing one in the near future. Remember, book sales attribute to me making a living and allows me to continue producing. Thank you for respecting my hard work and don't forget to subscribe to all of the other great things I'm doing on my YouTube channel, **Minimalist Vegan Lifestyle**.

Lastly, this book is not intended as a substitute for the medical advice of physicians. The reader should regularly consult a physician in matters relating to his/her health and particularly with respect to any symptoms that may require diagnosis or medical attention

# CONTENTS

**Introduction** 4

**Helpful Tips** 11

**Ingredients You May Not Be Familiar With** 12

**Homemade Sabor** 15 ~ Achiote Oil 17 ~ Sofrito 19 ~ Adobo 21 ~ Sazón 23

**Breakfast** 24 ~ Pineapple Mango Smoothie 26 ~ Papaya Coconut Smoothie 28 ~ Farina 30
~ Harina de Maiz 32 ~ Tofu Scramble 34 ~ Avocado Toast 36 ~ Roasted Potatoes 38 ~ Mangu de Platano 40
~ Mangu de Yuca 42

**Appetizers** 44 ~ Guava Crackers 46 ~ Guava Dip 48 ~ Plantain Chips 50 ~ Guacamole 50 ~ Empanadas de Carne 52

**Main Dishes** 56 ~ Black Bean Burger 58 ~ Jibarito 60 ~ Brown Rice 62 ~ Black Bean Stew and Pumpkin 64
~ Red Bean Stew and Plantain Balls 66 ~ Pink Bean Stew and Potatoes 68 ~ Arroz con Gandules 70
~ Arroz con Maiz 72 ~ Rice con Habichuelas 74 ~ Arroz con Vejetales 76 ~ Arroz sin Pollo 78 ~ Tvp Spaghetti 80
~ Pasteles 82

**Soups** 86 ~ Sopa de Platano 88 ~ Tofu Guisado 90 ~ Sopa de Gandules 92 ~ Sancocho 94

**Sides** 96 ~ Garlic Green Beans 98 ~ Cauliflower Achiote 100 ~ Baked Tostones 102 ~ Mayo Ketchup 102 ~ Plantain Fries 102
~ Yuca al Mojo 104 ~ Yuca Fries 106 ~ Potato Salad 108 ~ Macaroni Salad 110 ~ Lettuce Salad 112 ~ Spinach Salad 114

**Desserts** 116 ~ Tembleque 118 ~ Besito de Coco 120 ~ Sorullos 122 ~ Arroz con Leche 124
~ Guava Empanadas 126 ~ Pumpkin Empanadas 129 ~ Coconut Limber 132 ~ Pineapple Limber 132
~ Coconut Pineapple Limber 132 ~ Mantecaditos 134 ~ Guava Cheesecake 136

**Dimitri's Recipes** 138 ~ Tostones Rellenos 140 ~ Maduros 142 ~ Pastelon 144 ~ Canoas 147 ~ Albondigas 150
~ Pimientos Rellenos 152 ~ Guineo en Esacabeche 154 ~ Berenjenas Guisadas 156 ~ Quesitos 158

**Honerable Mentions** 161

# INTRODUCTION

Dear Reader,

You probably follow my YouTube Channel, Minimalist Vegan Lifestyle, where I've shared many Puerto Rican Vegan recipes and other aspects of my life. Some big changes are happening; I'm healing from agoraphobia, I'll be moving into a van, and I'll be getting married after 9 years. I needed to push myself every day to make sure this book could take its first breath. The trajectory of where I'm headed wouldn't support the space, electricity, and resources to give this book life otherwise. With that being said, the creation of this cookbook has given me purpose, connection, pride, joy, and has caused me to explore and express myself through these recipes.

Isn't it amazing how food can connect so many people across the globe? That no matter where two people are from, our cultures can still share the same ingredients, spices and cooking styles? Food helps us all share the same language and I love showcasing what we eat because it's so special to connect with you online. If you've asked me questions, left me suggestions, or encouraged me, then thank you, because I wouldn't be writing this without the courage of subscribers sharing pieces of themselves with me.

I want both my lifestyle and this book to inspire you in your own corner of the world. To inspire is to *infuse into the mind; to communicate to the spirit; to convey, as by a divine or supernatural influence; to disclose preternaturally; to produce in, as by inspiration.* This book is a tool to help you cook, but it should also be used as motivation to play in the kitchen, to have fun with your life, to always ask questions, and to always look towards bettering yourself.

*"I am because we are."* - African Proverb

My upbringing is where this cookbook began to write itself. I was born and raised in a Newark, NJ project complex and though I was bounced around in my youth, I mostly lived with a grandmother who couldn't read, write, or speak much English. Like many migrants of her generation, growing up in her town of

Luquillo, Puerto Rico, she dropped out of school at a very young age to help her parents take care of her siblings. Being a product of her household, I was culturally Puerto Rican because I was raised by someone who had traditions very close to the island and they were innately passed down to me.

We had our Latinx supermarkets, bodegas, piragueros, and our coco helado women. Salsa and bachata were often played on a big stereo with our back door open. Macarena was really big when I was a child, I played with dominoes, and I wore azabache jewelry and mal de ojos to ward off evil eyes. We still celebrated holidays the same way Puerto Rico did except the parrandas were in my madrina's tiny apartment and at home, we still had strict rituals with cooking and cleaning.

Despite being raised by the stereotypical Puerto Rican islander, I was still American because of basic TV, fast food, snacks, schooling, friends, and community. The demographics of my project complex was predominately Black minus one other Puerto Rican family, so many of my interests, references, and experiences come from Black American culture. We had big block parties, I was on a step team for parades, and I watched all the shows and listened to all of the music my friends did. So I was a part of the Puerto Rican New Years with the parrandas and the 12 grapes for good luck, but I also went to Black Baptist Churches, got my hair braided on the stoop, played hopscotch, jump rope, cards, and hand games. As a second generation Puerto Rican on the mainland, I wasn't aware of it, but I was working between two identities to invent my own.

We also grew up poor. I wore lots of hand-me downs from cousins and friends, and the adults did things like taking vinyl records and furniture out of the dumpster to furnish the house. With the lack of an income, what I remember most was how we ate. Our diet consisted of lots of canned meats, hot dogs, bologna, mac n' cheese, fried eggs (like boxed soup with an egg thrown in,) cereal, fried bacalaitos, plantains, white rice, and buttered bread with coffee. There were other foods available like soup with whole pieces of chicken in it but at a young age I could point out the blood, veins, cartilage, and nerve endings. As a child, I realized these things all too well and avoided them. In turn, I was so difficult to feed and I was consistently called picky and ungrateful. Their personal favorite phrase to tell me in these moments was, *pue, come mierda*, which translates to, "well, eat shit" a common saying among parents that was actually not meant to be as harsh as it sounds. This was just the way things were.

*"Knowledge is like a garden,*
*if it is not cultivated, it cannot be harvested."*
*- African Proverb*

By the time I was 14, I had an iron deficiency and was diagnosed with anemia. I was making poor health choices at a young age and it was affecting me. Looking back into my youth, I realize that I was always meant to be Vegan. I was sure animals were sentient, and because of that I tried to bring in every stray I saw in the projects even though I'd get yelled at because pets weren't allowed. By caring for them on this level, I had consciously made the connection that the "food" I was told to eat were living beings. I just didn't have the vocabulary or permission to understand myself in this way but it eventually found me through graphic videos on Facebook when I was 18 years old. This was the first time I heard about Veganism and I quickly went out to purchase a bunch of processed foods to look like the dishes I was told would make me feel good. Burgers, bacon, chicken, and cheeses. It was horrible! It was 2010 and the Vegan food wasn't where it is today so eventually, I failed because I didn't cook much and was living under someone else's roof.

I continued fighting against the idea of carnism. For so long we've been brainwashed into thinking we can go to a store to buy some caged parakeets to cherish while stopping by the poultry shop to pick a chicken to slaughter. After several attempts I successfully transitioned to Veganism 5 years later and I thrived when I found interesting ways to be a whole-foods plant-based Puerto Rican powerhouse. With a little bit of practice I started eating so many veganized versions of foods from the Puerto Rican cuisine of my youth and I was so happy! All those years of using the word *picky* to describe the undesirable feeling of biting into bones, seeing blood ooze out of my dish, the shredding of flesh, or the snapping back of a vein, were over. Right then and there, I knew that veganism choosing me was one of the best things that could happen.

The first recipes of this cookbook were brought to life when I asked my partner for new YouTube video suggestions and he said, "What about Puerto Rican Vegan Recipes? Show people all of our food," and of course, I was like, "No, I'll feel stupid. If you're Puerto Rican and Vegan you'll know how to make Puerto Rican Vegan food." At the time, I was still blinded by my own world of cooking so to meet him in the middle I originally made just one video with Puerto Rican Vegan food in it. It was called, **8 Puerto Rican Vegan Meals** and it's the most popular video on my channel.

To be clear, this wasn't the direction I was going in at all but I've come to realize that we are pulled in the direction we're needed. I developed a specific way of cooking and was already on a path of refining what I ate.

While I was going through my own journey, all of these messages were coming in and people needed help. They needed to see someone like them. They needed to have someone online to help them incite a change in their life. Some told me they wanted to be around their children longer, others were either transitioning to a Vegan diet or they were helping a family member do so. This called for an expansion of the first video, so out came a **Puerto Rican Vegan Meal Prep**, a **Puerto Rican Vegan Thanksgiving**, and a **Puerto Rican Vegan Christmas**.

Then I dug a little deeper and started experimenting with different recipe videos where there was an outpouring of more messages. Some people weren't Puerto Rican but their partners were, and others simply appreciated the cuisine. As I was being pulled more and more into recipe creating there was a reality being created for me: the art of intuitive cooking. I needed to change up my technique in order to show others what I was doing because in reality, we all intuitively cook. Intuitive cooking is the ability to cook our own food by seasoning to taste and adding our own liquids until it feels right. My job was to act as the example, to show you the bare minimum of what is expected in a dish, then you would be able to adjust the flavors to your liking.

> *"If you think you are too small to make a difference*
> *you haven't spent a night with a mosquito."*
> - African Proverb

But all of these great Vegan eats didn't come without backlash! Throughout my Vegan journey, many friends and YouTube commenters had the standard questions and comments about Veganism. Mostly people said, *it'll make you fat...* or *there's too many carbs...* Then there were those who would say, *oh, I could never stop eating meat...* and *but what about chicken... or fish... can I still eat that... cheese isn't an animal... what about eggs... I can't change... I love eating meat... it's so delicious... it has important nutrients... I've been doing it my whole life... there would be nothing left to eat...* In between conversations about high cholesterol and family members who were riddled with different cancers and health related diseases, I become saddened by these belief systems. Those who aren't attuned to a Vegan lifestyle can just shrug their shoulders and blame it on the *culture,* yet I refuse to entertain these excuses.

Individuals are not all to blame as many environments also try to make it difficult for those who want to live a healthy lifestyle. Some people don't live in areas where fruits and vegetables are in surplus, nor do some people have the economic means and knowledge to make a Vegan diet happen. There are plenty of people in the United States that live in food deserts, while others have the means to afford any kind of food they want, but don't make the best choices. Some have other things to worry about like air quality, drugs, or alcohol epidemics in their neighborhoods while others only struggle with deciding their next meal but lack the educational benefits of a plant based Vegan diet. All situations can leave our people nutritionally malnourished. What I'm trying to say is that everyone may not have access to Veganism because their socioeconomic systems may not be set up that way but Minimalist Vegan Lifestyle and this cookbook are my ways of being a part of the conversation.

*"If you want to go fast go alone.*
*If you want to go far go together."*
- African Proverb

The majority of us who decide to be plant based Vegan and see success are those that believe in the multitudes of ways that Veganism helps the planet and ourselves. Here are 11 reasons people choose Veganism.

1. To not participate in the exploitation, rape, mistreatment, or slaughtering of animals.
2. To pull money out of an industry with dangerous working conditions.
3. To take a stand against the mistreatment and commodification of the female body.
4. To cure & alleviate different symptoms, ailments, illnesses, and diseases.
5. To abstain from the consumption of fear, anxiety, and trauma.
6. To have a smaller environmental footprint with the reduction of air, water, and land pollution caused by the animal farming industry.
7. To increase one's spiritual connection.
8. To take athleticism to the next level.
9. To allow the body to detox and cleanse.
10. To save money.
11. To lose weight and feel lighter.

*"Not to know is bad. Not to desire to know is worse."* - African Proverb

My cookbook is not only a stamp on my Puerto Veganism but it also exposes people to some amazing traditional recipes with my minimalist spin. I love thinking about what my audience may not have access to so all throughout the book I sprinkle substitutions for the different kitchen products and ingredients. Instead of frying foods which are how most of these recipes are done, I boil and bake. Rather than using white rice, I use brown. You can also substitute your pasta and bread. I also teach you how to make our base spices from scratch because many people may not have access to the Adobo and Sazón or if you unexpectedly run out of it, you can always whip some up in a pinch. Additionally, it creates less waste and you avoid the extra anti-caking chemicals that are used in pre-made seasoning mixes.

Staying connected to the diaspora, another African Proverb mentions that *even the best cooking pot will not produce food*. It's important to note that you can make a lot happen with only a little. You will see that many of my recipes follow similar directions and there are only a handful of ingredients and products that only appear once. Our daily routines are important, and these recipes were made with those routines in mind. Lastly, many of these recipes can be frozen and are meal prep-able to add more simplicity to your life.

All in all, I thank you for listening to yourself and making the decision to purchase the **Puerto Rican Vegan Cookbook**. There are countless reasons why you could be reading this right now and I thank you for recognizing this book you hold in your hands. Whatever made you consider Veganism, I hope it makes you feel connected, yummy on the inside, and proud. As I always say, much love and abundance. Your health is in your hands. Make the necessary changes to feel amazing. Plant Power to the People!

CON MUCHO AMOR,
JACINIA PEREZ

# HELPFUL TIPS

1. For this book, I was cooking with an electric stove and oven. To save on electricity I didn't preheat my oven either. If you are used to preheating, be cautious when sticking to the bake times in the book.
2. If you still don't know what an ingredient is, refer to the next page for reference. I also have many older videos to accompany a lot of the recipes.
3. Read through the steps before starting a recipe to reduce confusion.
4. I always start my stove on high to medium high and then I lower to medium.
5. I almost always have my oven at 400 degrees.
6. When baking I always line my tray with compostable paper. This reduces the amount of oil needed.
7. Everything that is fried in traditional Puerto Rican cuisine is baked in this **Puerto Rican Vegan Cookbook**. Feel free to fry in oil or use an air fryer.
8. We don't eat olives in our household but olives are traditionally added to almost every savory dish. So if you love them, add them.
9. I only use brown rice. If you use white rice or any other grain, adjust your water accordingly.
10. When I add oil, I use grapeseed oil unless otherwise stated.
11. When I add a sweetener, it's either a vegan sugar or agave.
12. When I add flour, I'm using all purpose flour in this book. I usually use oat flour but it's an acquired texture.
13. When I add salt, I'm using Himalayan pink salt.
14. The most processed ingredients you'll find in this book are vegan butter, almond milk, cream cheese, tofu, and textured vegetable protein. You can make substitutions for these or add as many as you'd like.
15. You can reduce the amount of salt you use by substituting it with lemon or lime juice.
16. For a rolling pin, I used a pestle.
17. A food processor would be more functional than a blender for many recipes like picadillo, sofrito, and pasteles.
18. It's your kitchen and your body, you have total control over how you'd like to eat.

# INGREDIENTS YOU MAY NOT BE FAMILIAR WITH

Adobo- A seasoned salt used to marinate or season.

Sazón- A seasoned salt that adds a different color and flavor than adobo.

Sofrito- A blend of fresh fruits, vegetables, and herbs. Used as a wet sauce and loosely translates to *stir fry*.

Recao- Also known as: culantro, shado beni, bhandhania, chadron benee, coulante, and fit weed. If you don't have access to this, though not a direct substitute, you can double the cilantro.

Aji Dulce- Not to be confused with their spicy sibling the scotch bonnet, English speakers in the Caribbean call it seasoning pepper. Other names are ají cachucha, ajicito, and aji gustoso.

Annatto Seeds- Found from achiote trees, annatto seeds are used to add color and flavor.

Yuca- Also known as: manioc, macaxeira, mandioca, aipim is a starchy root vegetable that is typically boiled.

Yautia- Also called malanga, tannia, tannier, tanier, and cocoyam. It looks like a hairy yuca root while the inside is more slippery than a yuca root. Its flesh can be white, yellow, pink, or purple.

Cubanelle Pepper- also called Cuban pepper and Italian frying pepper. It has thin, wrinkly walls and is sweet with a slight hint of spice.

Ñame *(nyAH-may)*- Very large and rounded. Has creamy flesh that is softer than a potato with a nuttier flavor.

Batata- We can thank the Taíno for naming this. A batata is a sweet potato.

West Indian Pumpkin- Also known as calabaza and calabasa. It's a winter squash with skin varying from light green to dark yellow, and the flesh is sweet and bright orange. Other names are auyama, ayote, and zapallo.

Plantain- A starchy cooking banana that is sold individually. Plantains are typically large and can be found with green, yellow, or black skin. The fruit is light-yellow to yellow-orange. The more orange the fruit, the sweeter it is.

Green Banana- A starchy cooking banana that is sold in bunches. They are usually the size of a yellow banana. The flesh is typically white. Plantains and green bananas are not to be a substitute for one another.

# HOMEMADE SABOR

Most likely, you can purchase the spices necessary for these recipes at your local supermarket. Here are just some of the benefits of homemade seasoning:

- If your market doesn't sell these seasonings, you could always make it yourself.
- You avoid the harmful food additives.
- When you run out of seasoning you can always whip it up without having to go to the store.
- It saves you money to make it instead of paying brand name prices.

# Achiote Oil (Annatto Seed Oil)

½ cup (120 ml) oil
1 ¼ tbsp (19 ml) annatto seeds

1. Set pot to medium heat and add oil.
2. Add annatto seeds to the oil and stir.
3. When bubbles form in the oil, turn it off.
4. Strain the oil into a container and let it cool down before topping. Use within a week

Careful! If it's left for too long, the seeds will burn

and the oil will become bitter.

# Sofrito (means, "to stir- fry")

2 medium yellow onions
2 garlic bulbs
1 red pepper (traditionally, only green peppers are used but I like the varied nutrients a red pepper provides)
1 green pepper
1 recao
1 bunch of cilantro
10-12 ají dulce
1 cubanelle pepper (optional)

1. Wash all produce and roughly chop the green and red pepper leaving the stems and seeds behind.
2. Peel and quarter the onion.
3. De-stem the aji dulce and remove seeds. To remove seeds pinch the cap of the aji dulce and rip in half, then scrape the seeds out with your fingernail.
4. Peel the garlic cloves.
5. Chop the very end of the cilantro stems off.
6. Place all ingredients into a food processor and blend until finely minced.
7. In an airtight container, sofrito can keep in the refrigerator for about 2 weeks.

Use ice trays to portion. Once frozen,

store ice cubes in an airtight container to prevent freezer burn.

# Adobo

1 tbsp (15 ml) onion powder
1 tbsp (15 ml) turmeric
2 tbsp (30 ml) dried oregano
2 ½ tbsp (36 ml) salt
2 ½ tbsp (36 ml) garlic powder

1. Add all spices to a dry, empty jar. Attach the lid and shake.

If you have a spice grinder, use it to finely mince the spices. If not, shake before each use.

# Sazón

2 tsp (8 ml) cumin
2 tsp (8 ml) dried oregano
2 tsp (8 ml) dried cilantro
2 tsp (8 ml) ground coriander
2 tsp (8 ml) onion powder
2 tsp (8 ml) garlic powder
1 tbsp (15 ml) ground annatto

1.  Add all spices to a dry, empty jar. Attach the lid and shake.

If you are using lightly colored kitchenware or plastic,

sazón could cause red staining if it isn't soaked or washed quickly.

# BREAKFAST

For busy and nutritious breakfasts, smoothies are a go to. You can meal prep them and always have a
wonderful and affordable breakfast. On the weekends, it's nice to have heavier comfort foods.

# Pineapple Mango Smoothie

1 cup (240 ml) frozen mango chunks
2 ripe bananas
½ cup (120 ml) juice, plant milk, aloe vera juice, coconut water, or water
extras (protein powder, superfood powders, seeds, nuts oats, nut butters, greens)

1. Add frozen mango, liquid of choice, and peeled bananas to a blender.
2. Add in extras if desired.
3. Blend until smooth and creamy. Serve.

When you have extra time, make a smoothie bowl and eat it over a half hour period. Always add greens. To make a smoothie bowl, simply pour a thick smoothie into a bowl and add a variety of toppings like seeds, coconut flakes, nuts, dried fruit, granola, fresh fruit, and cinnamon.

# Papaya Coconut Smoothie

1 cup (240 ml) frozen papaya chunks
2 ripe bananas
½ cup (120 ml) coconut milk
sweetener of choice (optional)
extras (protein powder, superfood powders, seeds, nuts oats, nut butters, greens)

1. Add frozen papaya, coconut milk, sweetener, and peeled bananas to a blender.
2. Add in extras if desired.
3. Blend until smooth and creamy. Serve.

When you have extra time, make a fruit bowl. Add a variety of chopped fruit to a bowl and serve.

# Farina (Wheat Porridge)

1 ½ cups (350 ml) plant milk
½ cup (120 ml) water
3 tbsp (45 ml) sweetener
½ tsp vanilla extract
1/3 cup (80 ml) Farina, Cream of Wheat, or milled wheat
cinnamon, seeds, nuts, coconut flakes, dried fruit (optional)

1. Add milk, water, sweetener, and vanilla to a pot and stir until lightly boiling.
2. Add in farina slowly while stirring.
3. Stir continuously until the desired thickness is reached.
4. Pour into a bowl and add toppings. Serve.

Make sure that the pot is being stirred consistently.

If the porridge begins to pop, it will get lumpy.

# Harina de Maiz (Cornmeal Porridge)

1 ½ cups (350 ml) plant milk
½ cup (120 ml) water
3 tbsp (45 ml) sweetener
½ tsp (120 ml) vanilla extract
⅓ cup (80 ml) fine cornmeal
cinnamon, seeds, nuts, coconut flakes, dried fruit (optional)

1. Add milk, water, sweetener, and vanilla to a pot and stir until lightly boiling.
2. Add in corn meal slowly while stirring.
3. Stir continuously until desired consistency is reached.
4. Pour into a bowl and add toppings. Serve.

Harina de Maiz thickens quicker than Farina.

# Tofu Scramble

1 tbsp (15 ml) oil
½ cubed yellow onion
½ cubed red pepper
½ cubed green pepper
2 tbsp (30 ml) sofrito
1 tsp (5 ml) adobo
1 tsp (5 ml) sazón
½ tsp (2.5 ml) turmeric
½ tsp (2.5 ml) salt
8 oz (225 g) pressed firm tofu
4 cups (950 ml) chopped spinach

1. In a heated pan, saute onion with oil until translucent.
2. Toss peppers in and saute until caramelized.
3. Mix sofrito into the pan along with the spices.
4. Crumble tofu into the pan, mix until well combined.
5. Cook for 5-7 minutes. Stir occasionally.
6. Once desired texture is reached, add chopped spinach, mix well, and put the lid on with the burner off for 3 minutes or until spinach has wilted. Serve.

Place lid on for a moist tofu scramble or leave it uncovered for a crispy tofu scramble.

# Avocado Toast

8 slices of bread
1 ripe hass avocado
salt to taste
black pepper to taste
halved grape tomatoes
½ cup (120 ml) thinly sliced red onion

1. Cut 8 slices of bread diagonally to form triangles then place on a baking tray at 400 degrees for 5 minutes.
2. While the bread is toasting, slice tomatoes and onion.
3. Mash avocado in a separate bowl or directly onto your slices of toast.
4. Add onion and tomatoes.
5. Sprinkle salt and pepper to taste. Serve.

Swap out the bread for a slice of toasted sweet potato for a healthier alternative.

# Roasted Potatoes

4 cups (950 ml) cubed potatoes
1 tbsp (15 ml) oil (optional)
½ tsp (2.5 ml) smoked paprika
½ tsp (2.5 ml) dried oregano
½ tsp (2.5 ml) garlic powder
½ tsp (2.5 ml) onion powder

1. Cube potatoes. (The smaller you make the potatoes, the faster they will cook.)
2. Place cubed potatoes into a strainer and rinse.
3. Mix the potatoes, spices and oil in a bowl until all ingredients are coated evenly.
4. Place the seasoned potatoes on a baking tray at 400 degrees and bake for 40 minutes flipping halfway.
5. Add an additional 10 to 20 minutes if oil free.
6. Serve.

I leave the skin on the potatoes for extra nutrients!

# Mangu de Platano (Mashed Plantain)

2 quartered unripe plantains
½ tsp (2.5 ml) salt
⅓ cup (80 ml) cold water
1 tbsp (15 ml) vegan butter
½ to 1 chopped onion
1 tbsp (15 ml) oil
1 sliced red onion
½ tsp (2.5 ml) salt

1. Bring a medium pot of water to a boil.
2. Cut off the ends of the plantains and slit the peels lengthwise. Make sure to only slice the depth of the skin.
3. Take a knife and hold the plantain firmly with the sliced side facing you. Wedge the knife between the slice and move the knife to the left and right. This helps to remove the skin from the plantain. Do this from one side of the plantain to the other.
4. After putting your knife down, slide your thumbs under the skin until you've removed it from the plantain. Place peeled, quartered plantains into boiling water for 20 minutes.
5. Saute onion in a pan with oil and salt until caramelized.
6. Strain plantains and rinse with cold water to stop the cooking process.
7. Mash the plantains with water, butter, and salt.
8. Serve the mashed plantains with the sauteed onion.

# Mangu de Yuca (Mashed Cassava)

**YUCA**

1.5 lbs (681 g) frozen yuca
1 ½ tsp (7.5 ml) salt or to taste
1 tsp (5 ml) garlic powder
½ cup (120 ml) warm water
2 tbsp (30 ml) oil

**ONION**

½ to 1 chopped onion
1 tbsp (15 ml) oil
1 minced garlic clove
1 sliced red onion
½ tsp (2.5 ml) salt

1. Bring a medium pot of water to boil.
2. Place cassava into boiling water for 20 minutes or until fork tender.
3. Add oil to a pan. Saute garlic and onion until caramelized.
4. Strain cassava and reserve 1 cup of water.
5. Rinse cassava with cold water to prevent it from getting sticky and help it cool down.
6. Once cool to touch break cassava in half and pull out the woody roots.
7. Mash the cassava while slowly adding the reserved water until you reach a desired consistency.
8. Add salt and spices to taste and oil to reduce sticking.
9. Serve the cassava with the caramelized onions.

Yuca has a starchier consistency than plantains,

offset a sticky Mangu de Yuca with more oil and/or water.

# APPETIZERS

The perfect appetizer is fast, affordable, and beautiful. Many of these appetizers can be snacks, desserts, or sides.

# Guava Crackers

crackers
sliced guava paste
vegan cream cheese

1. Spread cream cheese onto a cracker.
2. Slice desired amount of guava and fit onto the cracker. Serve.

This is a fast and simple recipe that even children and shy kitchen goers can ace.

# Guava Dip

⅙ cup (40 ml) guava paste
⅓ cup (80 ml) vegan cream cheese

1. Combine guava and cream cheese and mash with a pestle and mortar or fork until you reach a whipped consistency. (tip: chop the guava into small pieces first)
2. Serve with sliced apples, bananas, kiwi, pretzels, or crackers.

This is one of my absolute favorite recipes in the book!

# Plantain Chips

2 unripe plantains, sliced ¼ inch thick
1 tbsp (15 ml) oil
salt to taste (optional)

1. Cut off the ends of the plantains and slit the peels lengthwise. Make sure to only slice the depth of the skin.
2. Take a knife and hold the plantain firmly with the sliced side facing you. Wedge the knife between the slice and move the knife to the left and right. This helps to remove the skin from the plantain. Do this from one side of the plantain to the other.
3. After putting your knife down, slide your thumbs under the skin until you've removed it from the plantain.
4. Now you can slice your plantain into ¼ inch discs.
5. Toss plantain chips in a bowl with oil and salt.
6. Lay them flat on a lined baking tray and bake at 400 degrees for 16 minutes, flipping them halfway. Serve.

# Guacamole

1 hass avocado
¼ tsp (1.25 ml) salt
¼ tsp (1.25 ml) black pepper
¼ cup (60 ml) diced tomato
¼ cup (60 ml) diced red onion
1 minced garlic clove
2 tbsp (30 ml) cilantro
1 tbsp (15 ml) lemon juice

1. Finely dice tomato and onion. Mince garlic clove and chop the cilantro. Add to a bowl.
2. Roll lemon to soften and create more juice. Cut in half and squeeze out your tablespoon worth of juice.
3. Slice avocado in half. Scoop into a bowl.
4. Mash the avocado and mix in the remaining ingredients. Serve.

# Empanadas de "Carne" (makes 12 Meatless Pies)

**TVP FILLING**
1 tsp (5 ml) oil
¼ cup (60 ml) sofrito
1 tsp (5 ml) adobo
1 tsp (5 ml) sazón
½ tsp (2.5 ml) black pepper
1 ½ cups (350 ml) tomato sauce
¾ cup (180 ml) textured vegetable protein

**DOUGH**
1 ¾ cups (410 ml) flour
½ tsp (2.5 ml) salt
6 tbsp (90 ml) fat (butter has better flavor, shortening has better texture)
1 tsp (5 ml) vinegar
½ cup (120 ml) cold water

**DOUGH**
1. In a large bowl, whisk together flour and salt. Using a pastry cutter or fork, cut in the fat until well combined. Avoid using hands as the warmth will begin to melt the fat and that is what gives the crust it's flaky texture.
2. Add cold water and vinegar, stirring with a fork. If the dough is still too dry add a tablespoon at a time and mix.
3. After the batter is well mixed, flour a flat surface and roll the dough out.
4. Fold the left side a third of the way over. Fold the right side a third of the way over. Fold the bottom a third of the way over. Fold the top a third of the way over. Repeat until it forms a cube.
5. Roll it out again, adding more flour if needed and repeat 5 times to create layers for a flaky dough.
6. Wrap tightly with plastic wrap and place in a container with a lid. Put it in the refrigerator for 1-2 hours.

Discs can be made one of two ways:
   a. Roll all the dough out to a desired thickness-- the sweet spot is 3/16 inches. Place a circular object on top of the dough like a lid and press down, it will cut through the dough. Repeat process with dough scraps.
   b. Separate the dough into equal sized spheres. Then, roll them out as circular as possible.
Freeze by stacking each disc on top of one another with parchment paper in between and store in an airtight container.

## FILLING

1. Heat oil in a separate pan and add sofrito, adobo, and sazón.
2. After 30 seconds mix in tomato sauce and black pepper.
3. Add textured vegetable protein, mix and top on medium heat for 4 minutes.
4. When finished, allow the tvp to cool down.
5. Take chilled dough out of the refrigerator and make discs.
6. Add 2-3 spoons of filling to the middle of the discs and fold over. Pinch the entire circumference about ½ inch deep with a fork.
7. Oil empanadas with a brush or your hand before placing them in the oven at 400 degrees for 30 minutes flipping halfway. Serve.

These empanadas are my biggest crowd pleasers

and have been known to be a "gateway dish" for non- vegans.

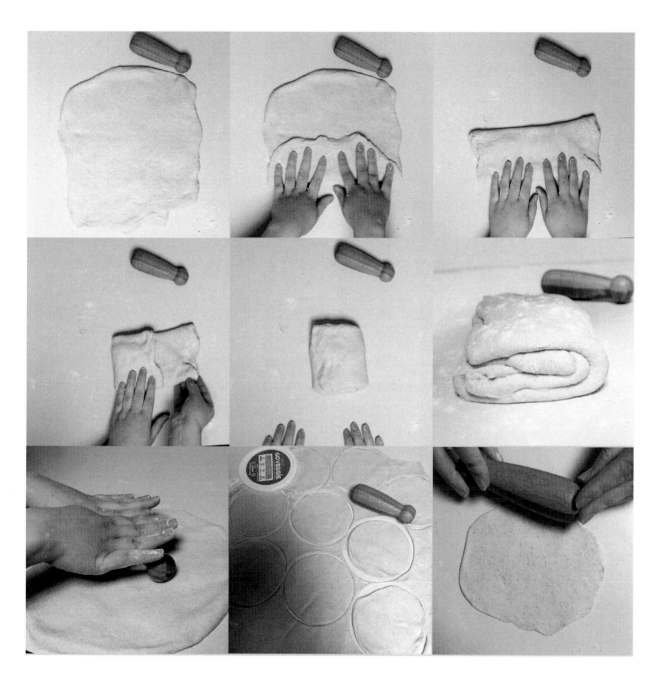

# MAIN DISHES

I am not afraid of carbohydrates, but always be sure to add many greens and vegetables to make more well rounded meals.

# Puerto Rican Black Bean Burger (makes 2 patties)

1 tbsp (15 ml) oil
3 tbsp (45 ml) sofrito
¾ tsp (3.5 ml) adobo
¾ tsp (3.5 ml) sazón
1 ½ cups (350 ml) black beans
2 tbsp (30 ml) flour, bread crumbs, or any starch alternative
½ tbsp (7.5 ml) baking powder
additional ingredients needed are bread, tomato, spinach, lettuce, red onion, mayo ketchup, guacamole

1. Heat oil in a pot and saute sofrito until fragrant.
2. Add in adobo, sazón, and beans.
3. Mix and mash most of the black beans into a paste with a fork or pestle.
4. Add flour and baking powder. Mix again, cooking for 2- 5 minutes.
5. Turn heat off and allow mixture to cool for 5 minutes.
6. Split mixture in half and add oil to your hands, forming the mixture into patties.
7. Place on a lined baking tray in the oven for 20 minutes at 400 degrees.
8. Flip burgers halfway through. Serve.

Try these on a grill press for a quick and crispy patty.

# Jibarito (Plantain Bread Sandwich)

3 unripe plantains, quartered
2- 4 tbsp (30- 60 ml) vegan butter
3 tbsp (45 ml) sofrito
¾ tsp (3.5 ml) adobo
¾ tsp (3.5 ml) sazón
8 oz (225 g) pressed firm tofu (optional: frozen and thawed. it's drier and "meatier" this way)
additional ingredient ideas are lettuce, spinach, tomato, onion, guacamole, and mayo ketchup

1. Bring water to boil and place peeled, quartered plantains in for 20 minutes.
2. Slice tofu into ⅛ inch slices or thicker.
3. Melt butter in a large pan and add sofrito, adobo, sazón, and tofu.
4. Saute on one side until crispy or cooked through. Flip and repeat. Takes 8 minutes.
5. Strain plantains and add oil to them in the same pot they were boiled in.
6. Place plantains on a lined baking tray and mash with a flat object like the bottom of a glass bowl.
7. Bake in the oven at 400 degrees for 40 minutes. Flip halfway.
8. Cut and prepare toppings and sides while you wait.
9. Assemble and serve.

Though the Jibarito sandwich dated back to the 90's, its origins are definitely paying tribute to the Jibaro; the iconic self- sustainable farm worker that made a living in the Puerto Rican countryside. Plantains were known to be their "daily bread."

# Plain Brown Rice

2 cups (475 ml) soaked brown rice
3 cups (700 ml) water
salt (optional)
oil (optional)

1. Soak rice for at least 30 minutes.
2. Add water, oil, and salt to a pot. Bring to a boil.
3. Add strained rice to the pot. Set the fire to medium high.
4. Boil the water down until it's levelled with the rice.
5. Once bubbles are forming through the rice, cover, and set the stove to medium.
6. After 30 minutes, remove the lid and mix.
7. If the rice needs more water or needs to cook longer now is the time to make adjustments.
8. Once it reaches desired softness, turn off and serve.

Remember: frozen rice is very versatile. It could be thrown in a soup

or used later in a dessert like Arroz con Leche on page 124.

# Black Bean and Pumpkin Stew

1 tsp (5 ml) oil
3 tbsp (45 ml) sofrito
1 tsp (5 ml) adobo
1 tsp (5 ml) sazón
5 tbsp (75 ml) tomato sauce
1 ½ cups (350 ml) black beans
1 cup (240 ml) water
1- 1 ½ cups (240- 350 ml) West Indian pumpkin

1. After heating oil in a pot, add sofrito, adobo, and sazón.
2. Mix in the tomato sauce, beans, and water.
3. While waiting for it to boil, cut the skin off the pumpkin and remove the seeds. Then cut the pumpkin into 1- 1 ½ inch cubes.
4. When the bean stew comes to a boil add the cubed pumpkin, mix, and top on medium heat.
5. After 7 minutes, check the hardness of the pumpkin. When the pumpkin is cooked through, serve.

If you do not have access to pumpkin, try sweet potato.

# Red Beans and Plantain Ball Stew

1 tsp (5 ml) oil
3 tbsp (45 ml) sofrito
1 tsp (5 ml) adobo
1 tsp (5 ml) sazón
5 tbsp (75 ml) tomato sauce
1 ½ cups (350 ml) red beans
1 cup (240 ml) water

## PLANTAIN BALLS
1 grated unripe plantain
1 minced garlic

1. After heating oil in a pot, add sofrito, adobo, and sazón.
2. Mix in the tomato sauce, beans, and water.
3. While waiting for the water to boil, peel and finely grate the plantain and garlic.
4. Mix the plantain and garlic well and form into balls.
5. When the bean stew comes to a boil add in the plantain balls and mix gently. Top with a lid on medium heat.
6. When the plantain balls float and/or are cooked through, serve.

Make your add-ins smaller for a quicker pot of beans.

# Pink Beans and Potato Stew

1 tsp (5 ml) oil
3 tbsp (45 ml) sofrito
1 tsp (5 ml) adobo
1 tsp (5 ml) sazón
5 tbsp (75 ml) tomato sauce
1 ½ cups (350 ml) pink beans
1 cup (240 ml) water
1 medium potato, cubed

1. After heating oil in a pot, add sofrito, adobo, and sazón.
2. Mix in the tomato sauce, beans, and water.
3. Once the beans boil, add in cubed potatoes.
4. The beans are ready to plate once the potatoes are soft.

You can add in other delicious foods like green banana,

sweet potato, carrot, spinach, kale, and corn.

# Arroz con Gandules (Rice with Pigeon Peas)

1 tbsp (15 ml) oil
3 tbsp (45 ml) sofrito
1 ½ tsp (7.5 ml) adobo
1 ½ tsp (7.5 ml) sazón
½ tsp (2.5 ml) salt
⅓ cup (80 ml) tomato sauce
2 ¾ cups (650 ml) water
1 ½ cups (350 ml) soaked brown rice
1 ½ cups (350 ml) pigeon peas

1. Soak rice for at least 30 minutes.
2. After heating up oil in a pot, add sofrito, adobo, and sazón and heat through.
3. Mix in the tomato sauce, gandules, and water.
4. Once the pot begins to boil, throw in strained rice and add salt.
5. Boil the water down until it's levelled with the rice. It should take about 25 minutes.
6. Once bubbles are forming through the rice, put the lid on and set the stove to medium.
7. Check the rice about 30 minutes later. If the rice needs to be adjusted, add water.
8. Serve once it reaches your desired softness.

Pigeon peas ARE NOT green peas or black eyed peas. They can typically be found in the international section at your local supermarket. This meal is popular around Christmas, but why not have it year round?

# Arroz con Maiz (Rice with Corn)

1 tbsp (15 ml) oil
3 tbsp (45 ml) sofrito
1 ½ tsp (7.5 ml) adobo
1 ½ tsp (7.5 ml) sazón
½ tsp (2.5 ml) salt
⅓ cup (80 ml) tomato sauce
2 ¾ cups (650 ml) water
1 ½ cups (350 ml) soaked brown rice
2 cups (475 ml) frozen corn

1. Soak rice for at least 30 minutes.
2. After heating up oil in a pot, add sofrito, adobo, and sazón and heat through.
3. Mix in the tomato sauce, corn, and water.
4. Once the pot begins to boil, throw in strained rice and add salt.
5. Boil the water down until it's levelled with the rice. It should take about 25 minutes.
6. Once bubbles are forming through the rice, put the lid on and set the stove to medium.
7. Check the rice about 30 minutes later. If the rice needs to be adjusted, add water.
8. Serve once it reaches your desired softness.

Corn adds a sweetness to this rice, not to mention making it affordable and accessible to all.

# Arroz con Habichuelas (Rice with Beans)

1 tbsp (15 ml) oil
3 tbsp (45 ml) sofrito
1 ½ tsp (7.5 ml) adobo
1 ½ tsp (7.5 ml) sazón
½ tsp (2.5 ml) salt
⅓ cup (80 ml) tomato sauce
2 ¾ cups (650 ml) water
1 ½ cups (350 ml) soaked brown rice
1 ½ cups (350 ml) any bean

1. Soak rice for at least 30 minutes.
2. After heating up oil in a pot, add sofrito, adobo, and sazón and heat through.
3. Mix in the tomato sauce, bean of choice, and water.
4. Once the pot begins to boil, throw in strained rice and add salt.
5. Boil the water down until it's levelled with the rice. It should take about 25 minutes.
6. Once bubbles are forming through the rice, put the lid on and set the stove to medium.
7. Check the rice about 30 minutes later. If the rice needs to be adjusted, add water.
8. Serve once it reaches your desired softness.

Beans are great for adding more nutrients than corn. You can use any bean you like. If you add black beans you'll have a popular Cuban and Dominican dish called Moro, or Congris. Congris, or Moro both use easy to find ingredients and could be seen on my YouTube Channel.

# Arroz con Vejetales (Rice with Vegetables)

1 tbsp (15 ml) oil
3 tbsp (45 ml) sofrito
1 ½ tsp (7.5 ml) adobo
1 ½ tsp (7.5 ml) sazón
½ tsp (2.5 ml) salt
⅓ cup (80 ml) tomato sauce
2 ¾ cups (650 ml) water
1 ½ cups (350 ml) soaked brown rice
2 cups (350 ml) frozen mixed vegetables

1. Soak rice for at least 30 minutes.
2. After heating up oil in a pot, add sofrito, adobo, and sazón and heat through.
3. Mix in the tomato sauce, mixed vegetables, and water.
4. Once the pot begins to boil, throw in strained rice and add salt.
5. Boil the water down until it's levelled with the rice. It should take about 25 minutes.
6. Once bubbles are forming through the rice, put the lid on and set the stove to medium.
7. Check the rice about 30 minutes later. If the rice needs to be adjusted, add water.
8. Serve once it reaches your desired softness.

This is a very unpopular dish but I love to make it. The different vegetables create a complex flavor and I love all of the textures.

# Arroz sin Pollo (Rice without Chicken)

2 tbsp (30 ml) vegan butter
3 tbsp (45 ml) sofrito
1 ½ tsp (7.5 ml) adobo
1 ½ tsp (7.5 ml) sazón
½ tsp (2.5 ml) salt
⅓ cup (80 ml) tomato sauce
2 ¾ cups (650 ml) water
1 ½ cups (350 ml) soaked brown rice
8 oz (225 g) pressed firm tofu (frozen and thawed)

1. After heating butter in a pot, add sofrito, adobo, and sazón and heat through.
2. Add in cubed tofu and crisp.
3. Mix in the tomato sauce and water.
4. Once boiling, throw in drained rice and salt.
5. After 25 minutes or when bubbles are forming through the rice, put the lid on and set the stove to medium.
6. After 30 minutes mix the rice. Add more water or cook longer if needed.
7. Serve once desired softness is reached.

Be sure your tofu is frozen and pressed, if not it will break apart during the cooking process.

# TVP Spaghetti

1 tsp (5 ml) oil
¼ cup (60 ml) sofrito
1 tsp (5 ml) adobo
1 tsp (5 ml) sazón
½ tsp (2.5 ml) black pepper
1 ½ cups (350 ml) tomato sauce
½ cup (120 ml) textured vegetable protein for a Saucy Picadillo Recipe

or…

¾ cup (180 ml) textured vegetable protein for Chunky Picadillo Recipe
8 oz (240 ml) boiled pasta

1. Boil pasta until al dente.
2. Heat oil in a separate pan and add sofrito, adobo, and sazón.
3. After 30 seconds mix in tomato sauce and black pepper.
4. Add textured vegetable protein, mix and top on medium heat for 4 minutes.
5. Strain pasta, mix in with the sauce. Serve.

If you do not have access to tvp, try substituting with beans, tofu, quinoa, or vegan crumbles.

[Puerto Rican Vegan Cookbook] 82

# Pasteles (Puerto Rican Tamales)

**TVP PICADILLO**
1 tsp (5 ml) oil
¼ cup (60 ml) sofrito
1 tsp (5 ml) adobo
1 tsp (5 ml) sazón
½ tsp (2.5 ml) black pepper
1 ½ cups (350 ml) tomato sauce
¾ cup (180 ml) textured vegetable protein

**MASA FOR 1 DOZEN PASTELES**
6 green bananas
1 large unripe plantain
1 lb (455 g) West Indian pumpkin
1 lb (455 g) yautia
1 medium potato
5 tbsp (75 ml) annatto oil
adobo to taste
salt to taste
vegetable broth to taste

1. Heat oil in a separate pan and add sofrito, adobo, and sazón.
2. After 30 seconds mix in tomato sauce and black pepper.
3. Add textured vegetable protein, mix and top on medium heat for 4 minutes.
4. Peel and roughly chop your medium potato. Add it to a food processor.
5. Cut the skin off the pumpkin and scoop the seeds out. If there is some green left on the pumpkin after cutting the skin off, you can peel it with a vegetable peeler.
6. Roughly chop the pumpkin and add it to the food processor.
7. Chop off the ends of the yautia and peel with a vegetable peeler.
8. Roughly chop the yautia and add it to the food processor.
9. Next, rub some oil in your hands to prevent staining. Cut off the ends of the plantains and green banana. Then, slit the peels lengthwise. Place your knife along the sliced area and pop your knife to the left and right, removing the peel from the fruit.

10. Glide your thumb along the line to remove the rest of the peel. Roughly chop and add to the food processor.
11. To help the food processor blend, add vegetable broth and oil. Blend until there are no more chunks.
12. Add to a bowl and mix in adobo and salt.

## ASSEMBLY

1. Place pastel paper, aluminum foil, parchment paper, or banana leaf on counter. Add one tablespoon of annatto oil in the center.
2. Spoon dough on top of the oil. Shape it into a rectangle and use the large cooking spoon to make a dip the shape of an oval in the middle of the masa. This is where you can add the picadillo and other ingredients. Add however much picadillo fits in the dip.
3. Next, fold over the pastel paper with the longer side facing you. The dough should now be folded in half and completely closed.
4. Gently smooth the top of the pastel once folded. Then glide your hand across the pastel paper on three sides, creating sealed edges.
5. Fold the longest end of the paper at one inch and keep folding until you're able to fold that end over and have it be in the very center of the pastel.
6. Now fold the shorter ends 2 times each making sure it's completely sealed.
7. Set pastel aside with the folded portion face down while the next pastel is prepared.
8. Repeat steps 1-8 until all pasteles are folded and secure.
9. Before tying 2 together, pasteles should have folded sides facing each other.
10. Cut a piece of string and form a long u shape, sliding it under the pasteles.
11. Hold the bottom of the u open with your index finger and thumb and with your other hand grab the two legs of the u and pull it through the loop between your finger and thumb.
12. Pull the two ends of the string to one end of each pastel so that it now makes an H shape.
13. Flip the pasteles over and tie those two ends together.
14. Repeat until all 12 are finished.
15. Boil them in salted water for 40 minutes with the paper on or freeze to cook later.
16. To serve, pull it out of the water when done cooking, cut the string, unravel the paper, and place your pasteles on a plate.

# SOUPS

One pot meals are some of my favorite dishes as a minimalist. With a variety of textures and flavors, these meals can be as simple or as complex as you want while still packing a nutritious punch.

# Sopa de Platano (Plantain Soup)

1 tbsp (15 ml) annatto oil
3 minced garlic cloves
1 small chopped onion
½ tsp (2.5 ml) salt
½ tsp (2.5 ml) black pepper
5 cups (1190 ml) vegetable broth
2 unripe grated plantains

1. Peel and mince garlic. Peel and dice onion.
2. Add oil to a medium high pan. When heated, add garlic and cook until fragrant. Then, throw onion in and cook until transparent or caramelized.
3. Add in vegetable broth, salt, and pepper to taste.
4. Cut off the ends of the plantains then slit the peels lengthwise. Place knife along the sliced area and pop it to the left and right, removing the peel from the fruit. Finely grate the plantain.
5. Once broth reaches a boil add in the grated plantain. When water comes back to a boil, set to medium heat for 20 minutes. Serve.

This soup does not do well as a leftover, so to help you finish this in one sitting, add some cubed avocado for extra flavor.

# Tofu Guisado (Tofu Stew)

1 tbsp (15 ml) oil
2 ½ tbsp (37.5 ml) sofrito
1 tsp (5 ml) sazón
1 tsp (5 ml) adobo
½ tsp (2.5 ml) dried oregano
1 tsp (5 ml) ground cumin
½ pressed frozen thawed tofu, cubed
2 carrots, sliced into discs
2 potatoes, cubed
½ cup (120 ml) tomato sauce
5 cups (1190 ml) water
1 tbsp (15 ml) vegetable broth

1. Slice carrots, cube potatoes and cube tofu.
2. After heating oil in a pot, add sofrito and tofu.
3. Mix up, add spices, and crisp.
4. Add tomato sauce and saute for 2-3 minutes.
5. Add carrots and potatoes.
6. Add vegetable broth and boil on medium with the lid on for 30 minutes or until soft. Serve.

This is a very liquidy soup. You Can make it thicker by blending some of it.

# Asopao de Gandules (Pigeon Pea Soup)

1 tbsp (15 ml) oil
¾ cup (180 ml) chopped onion
1 ¾ cups (410 ml) sliced carrots
1 cup (240 ml) tomato sauce
1 tsp (5 ml) adobo
1 tsp (5 ml) sazón
½ tsp (2.5 ml) salt
½ tsp (2.5 ml) black pepper
½ tsp (2.5 ml) cumin
¼ tsp (1.25 ml) dried oregano
1 tbsp (15 ml) vegetable broth
6 cups (1400 ml) water
3 cups (700 ml) pigeon peas
½ cup (120 ml) soaked brown rice
1 unripe grated plantain
1 grated garlic clove

1. Peel and chop onion.
2. In a large pot, heat oil through on medium high. Then add chopped onion and saute.
3. Wash, peel, and chop carrots into slices and saute.
4. Add tomato sauce, spices, water, pigeon peas, and vegetable broth.
5. Once boiling, strain rice and add it to the pot.
6. While the pot boils, peel and finely grate garlic and plantain. Form mixture into balls and add them to the pot.
7. Put the lid on and cook on medium heat for 20 minutes or until the plantain balls float. Serve.

This soup is great for using leftover rice. If you don't have any precooked rice use uncooked soaked rice.

# Sancocho (Tuber and Root Vegetable Stew)

1 tbsp (15 ml) oil
½ cup (120 ml) sofrito
1 tbsp (15 ml) sazón
1 tbsp (15 ml) adobo
½ cup (120 ml) tomato sauce
1 tbsp (15 ml) vegetable broth
5 cups (1180 ml) water
2 bay leaves
1 yuca
1 yautia
1 batata
1 ñame
1 unripe plantain
1 potato
4 mini corn on the cobs chopped into discs
1 ½ lb (680 g) West Indian pumpkin

1. Slice corn into fourths and set aside.
2. Spoon seeds out of pumpkin and chop skin off with knife. Peel any imperfect spots on the pumpkin with a vegetable peeler. Cube and set aside.
3. Heat oil in a large pot. When heated through mix in sofrito, adobo, and sazón. Add tomato sauce, vegetable broth, water, and bay leaves.
4. While waiting for your broth to boil, wash and cube the potato and set aside.
5. Chop ends of plantain off and slice the skin from end to end so you can remove the peel from the plantain. Slice and set aside.
6. Chop ends off of yuca, yautia, and batata. Peel, chop and set aside.
7. Peel and cube ñame and set aside.
8. When the broth has come up to a boil, place in all ingredients.
9. Lower stove to medium and top for 50 minutes or until every ingredient is cooked through.
10. Pull bay leaves out before serving.

# SIDES

Most of these sides are classics for holidays. For everyday meals, they add variety and color to your plate.

# Garlic and Green Beans

1 tbsp (15 ml) oil
6 minced garlic cloves
5 cups (1180 ml) green beans
1 tsp (5 ml) salt
1 ½ tsp (7.5 ml) garlic powder

1. Peel and mince garlic cloves.
2. Heat oil in a pan for 30 seconds and drop in the minced garlic.
3. After 30 seconds mix in green beans.
4. Mix in spices and saute on medium for 10 minutes.
5. For the last 5 minutes cover with lid. Stir and serve.

If you don't like green beans, this recipe works great with broccoli.

# Cauliflower Achiote

½ tsp (2.5 ml) salt
½ tsp (2.5 ml) black pepper
1 tsp (5 ml) garlic powder
2 tbsp (30 ml) annatto oil
1 ½ (350 ml) cups chopped cauliflower

1. While the oven is preheating wash and chop cauliflower into florets.
2. Add the cauliflower to a bowl with oil, salt, black pepper, and garlic.
3. Place cauliflower on a lined baking tray and cook for 30 minutes at 400 degrees mixing halfway. Serve.

Alternatively, cut cauliflower head into steaks and brush the oil and seasoning on. This makes for less chopping, saving you time in the kitchen.

# Baked Tostones (Baked Double Fried Plantains)

1 unripe plantain
3 tbsp (45 ml) oil (half on one side, half on the other)

1. While oven is preheating, cut off the ends of the plantains. Then, slit the peels lengthwise. Place your knife along the sliced area and pop your knife to the left and right, removing the peel from the fruit.
2. Glide your thumb along the line to remove the rest of the peel and cut into 1 inch thick discs.
3. Place plantain discs into a bowl with oil and mix in spices.
4. Place on a lined baking tray for 400 degrees at 20 minutes.
5. Take them out and toss in a bowl with remaining oil and smash with a tostonera or between two hard surfaces like a cutting board and bottom of a bowl.
6. Bake at 400 degrees for an additional 20 minutes. Serve.

# Mayo Ketchup

2 tbsp (30 ml) vegan mayonnaise
2 tbsp (30 ml) ketchup
¼ tsp (1.25 ml) garlic powder
⅛ tsp (.75 ml) black pepper

1. Add all ingredients into a bowl and mix.
2. Adjust by adding more or less of any ingredient to taste.
3. This condiment can stay fresh in an airtight container as long as ketchup and mayonnaise can.

# Plantain Fries

2 unripe plantains cut into sticks
1 tbsp (15 ml) oil
spices (optional)

1. While the oven is preheating, cut off the ends of the plantains then slit the peels lengthwise. Place your knife along the sliced area and pop your knife to the left and right, removing the peel from the fruit.
2. Glide your thumb along the line to remove the rest of the peel.
3. Cut into sticks.
4. Toss plantain fries in a bowl with oil and spices.
5. Place on a lined baking tray at 400 degrees for 30 minutes flipping halfway. Serve.

# Yuca al Mojo (Cassava with Garlic Sauce)

1 ½ lbs (680 g) yuca
6 tbsp (90 ml) oil
1 sliced onion
2 minced garlic cloves
2 tsp (10 ml) lemon juice
½ tsp (2.5 ml) salt
½ tsp (2.5 ml) black pepper

1. Set water to boil in a large pot.
2. While waiting, mash garlic cloves with a mortar and pestle or mince garlic.
3. Add the remaining ingredients to the garlic and allow the sauce to marinade.
4. Add yuca to the pot on medium high for 20 minutes.
5. Strain and allow to cool.
6. Pull yucas apart exposing its root and pull it out.
7. Add sauce to yuca and let it marinade.

I always eat this immediately, but it's even more delicious the longer you let it marinate. If you decide to serve it the next day, add bay leaves to the oil.

# Yuca Fries (Cassava Fries)

1 ½ cups (360 ml) yuca
1 tbsp (15 ml) oil
½ tsp (2.5 ml) garlic powder
¼ tsp (1.25 ml) salt
¼ tsp (1.25 ml) black pepper

1. Bring water to boil in a pot.
2. While waiting, cut yuca into sticks. I usually cut out the area in the very center.
3. Add yuca to the boiling water on medium high heat for 10- 12 minutes.
4. Strain yuca and rinse under cold water to prevent stickiness.
5. Throw fries into a bowl with oil and spices.
6. Place fries onto a lined baking tray being sure not to overcrowd.
7. Bake for 30 minutes at 400 degrees, flipping halfway. Serve.

These yuca fries pair well with the Mojo on page 104.

# (Ensalada de Papa) Potato Salad

4 cups (950 ml) diced potatoes
¼ cup (60 ml) diced red onion
⅓ cup (80 ml) diced celery
¼ cup (60 ml) vegan mayonnaise
¾ tsp (3.75 ml) salt
½ tsp (2.5 ml) black pepper
1 minced garlic clove

1. Boil water in a pot.
2. While waiting, wash, peel and cube potatoes.
3. While the potatoes are boiling you can wash and chop celery. Peel and mince the garlic and onion.
4. Strain potatoes when tender and allow to cool before adding the mayonnaise, vegetables, and spices.
5. Eat it right away or set it in the refrigerator to cool for later.

If vegan mayonnaise is difficult to come by in your area, do a web search. There are many DIY mayo recipes using hemp seeds, tofu, plant milk, etc.

# (Ensalada de Macarrones) Macaroni Salad

16 oz (455 g) pasta
½ cup (120 ml) diced red pepper
¼ cup (60 ml) diced red onion
⅓ cup (80 ml) diced celery
¼ cup (60 ml) vegan mayonnaise
¾ tsp (3.75 ml) salt
½ tsp (2.5 ml) black pepper
¼ tsp (1.25 ml) turmeric
1 minced garlic clove

1. Boil water in a pot.
2. While waiting for the pasta to boil, wash and chop celery and pepper. Peel and mince the garlic and onion.
3. Strain pasta when tender and allow to cool before adding the mayonnaise, vegetables, and spices.
4. Eat it right away or set it in the refrigerator to cool for later.

In this photo, I used flour pasta, but my favorite is brown rice pasta.

# Lettuce Salad

½ hass avocado
½ tsp (2.5 ml) salt
2 tbsp (30 ml) lemon juice
5 tbsp (75 ml) water
1-2 tbsp (15-30 ml) chopped fresh cilantro
¼ cup (60 ml) chopped red onion
¼ cup (60 ml) diced tomato
8 oz (225 g) lettuce
shredded cabbage and carrots (optional)

1. Add half an avocado, salt, lemon juice, and water to a blender and blend until creamy.
2. Add vegetables and lettuce to a bowl and cover with avocado dressing. Serve.

This salad dressing can stay fresh for 2 days because the lemon juice keeps it from browning. Use it in an upcoming meal prep.

# Spinach Salad

8 oz (225 g) baby spinach
1 hass avocado
½ tsp (2.5 ml) salt
2 tbsp (30 ml) lemon juice
¼ cup (60 ml) diced red onion
¼ cup (60 ml) diced red pepper
¼ cup (60 ml) shredded carrot
¼ cup (60 ml) diced tomato

1. Add chopped or whole baby spinach to a bowl.
2. Wash carrot, red pepper, and tomato before chopping/ shredding and add to the bowl.
3. Halve an avocado and slice it into small cubes.
4. Scoop diced avocado into a bowl and mix in lemon juice and salt. Serve.

This is one of our most often eaten meals during the summer months where we also add black beans and sautéed peppers to it.

[Puerto Rican Vegan Cookbook] 116

# DESSERTS

Many people say that desserts should be eaten in moderation, but sometimes that's difficult for us to do. To curb temptation, I think it's helpful to turn to homemade treats so you can know and control the ingredients going into your body. Some of these recipes are so cheap and easy you can practically make them every day.

# Tembleque (Coconut Custard)

2 cans full- fat coconut milk
½ cup (120 ml) starch
¼ tsp (1.25 ml) salt
½ cup (120 ml) sweetener

1. Dump two cans of coconut milk into a sauce pan and add sugar and salt while stirring.
2. Put cold water into the mold you'll be using and set aside.
3. Slowly sift and vigorously whisk in starch.
4. Stir with a spoon on medium heat for 15 minutes until thick and slightly transparent.
5. Once thickened, pour water out of the mold while leaving about a teaspoon behind. Pour in the coconut mixture.
6. Cool on the counter and set in the fridge until thick, usually overnight.
7. Once completely cooled slide a butter knife around the edges and flip over onto a plate.
8. Sprinkle with cinnamon and serve.

Although flan is my favorite custard, I always choose to make tembleque. It's easy, minimalist, and requires very little time.

# Besitos de Coco (Coconut Kisses)

2 cups (475 ml) coconut flakes
½ cup (120 ml) condensed milk

to make Vegan condensed milk:
      a.  1 can of full- fat coconut milk
      b.  ⅓ c (80 ml) sweetener
      c.  Stir in pot until it thickens and becomes clearer- about 40 minutes

1 cup (240 ml) flour
1 tsp (5 ml) vanilla extract
pinch of salt (optional)

1. Make condensed milk and set aside.
2. Sift flour and salt into a bowl.
3. Mix in condensed milk, vanilla, and coconut flakes until well combined.
4. Sprinkle a thin layer of flour on a lined baking tray.
5. Use a scoop or spoon to form them into macaroons and set them on the tray.
6. Bake at 375 degrees for 20 minutes, keeping a close eye on them. If the flakes become browned, take out early.
7. Serve.

Some people add a piece of guava in the center. These are sweet as is, but I'm sure the combination of coconut and guava is amazing.

# Sorullos (Cornmeal Sticks)

¾ cup (180 ml) fine cornmeal
2 tbsp (30 ml) sweetener
¼ tsp (1.25 ml) salt
1 tbsp (15 ml) vegan butter
1 cup (240 ml) water
1 tsp (5 ml) baking powder
agave or maple syrup for brushing
sugar for sprinkling

1. Heat water, butter, salt, and sugar in a pot.
2. Once ingredients come to a light boil, add baking powder and stir. Then, slowly add in the cornmeal, stirring constantly.
3. Once the cornmeal starts to form a dough ball turn off heat and continue stirring until a neat ball forms.
4. Spread dough ball on a plate to cool.
5. When dough is cool enough to handle, form it into rods and place them on a lined baking tray.
6. Brush agave on both sides and sprinkle sugar on top or roll cornmeal sticks in a bowl to get the sugar on.
7. Bake at 400 degrees for 30 minutes flipping halfway. Serve.

I ate these so much as a child and always had them with sugar, but they are also served without sugar and accompanied with Mayo Ketchup. That recipe is on page 102.

# Arroz con Leche (Rice Pudding)

3 cups (700 ml) cooked brown rice
½ tsp (2.5 ml) vanilla extract
½ tsp (2.5 ml) cinnamon
1 can full- fat coconut milk
¼ cup (60 ml) sweetener
ginger, cloves, lemon orange zest (optional)

1. Add coconut milk or vanilla, cinnamon, sugar, and any optional ingredients to a saucepan. Stir.
2. Once boiling, add in cooked rice.
3. Boil for 8 minutes with the lid on or until you reach your desired consistency.
4. Once cooled on the counter, set in refrigerator until cold.
5. Sprinkle cinnamon on top. Serve.

These are one of the recipes where you can really make it your own. People typically add anise, cloves, cinnamon sticks, raisins, etc.

# Guava Empanadas (makes 12)

**DOUGH**
1 3/4 cups (410 ml) flour
¼ tsp (1.25 ml) salt
1 tsp (5 ml) vinegar
½ cup (120 ml) cold water
6 tbsp (90 ml) fat (butter has better flavor but shortening has better texture.)
1 tsp cinnamon (5 ml)

**GUAVA FILLING**
sliced guava paste
vegan cream cheese

**DOUGH**
1. In a large bowl, mix flour and salt. Using a pastry cutter or fork, cut in the fat until it has the texture of chunky sand. Avoid using hands as the warmth will begin to melt the fat and that is what gives the crust it's flaky texture.
2. Add cold water and vinegar, stirring with a fork. If the dough is still too dry add a tablespoon at a time and mix.
3. After the batter is well mixed, flour a flat surface and roll the dough out.
4. Fold the left side a third of the way over. Fold the right side a third of the way over. Fold the bottom a third of the way over. Fold the top a third of the way over. Repeat until it forms a cube.
5. Roll it out again, adding more flour if needed and repeat 5 times to create layers for a flaky dough.
6. Wrap tightly with plastic wrap and place in a container with a lid. Put it in the refrigerator for 1-2 hours.

Discs can be made one of two ways:
1. Roll all the dough out to a desired thickness-- the sweet spot is 3/16 inches. Place a circular object on top of the dough like a lid and press down, it will cut through the dough. Repeat process with dough scraps.
2. Separate the dough into equal sized spheres. Then, roll them out as circular as possible.
Freeze by stacking each disc on top of one another with parchment paper in between and store in an airtight container.

**ASSEMBLY**
1. Take a spoonful of vegan cream cheese and sliced guava paste and place it to the side of the center of the disc.
2. Fold in half and press the very edge of the circumference down with a fork.
3. Flip over and repeat. They should look like half moons.
4. Poke the top of the empanada with a fork.
5. Brush the top with almond milk.
6. Place on a lined backing tray and bake at 400 degrees for 30 minutes, flipping halfway.

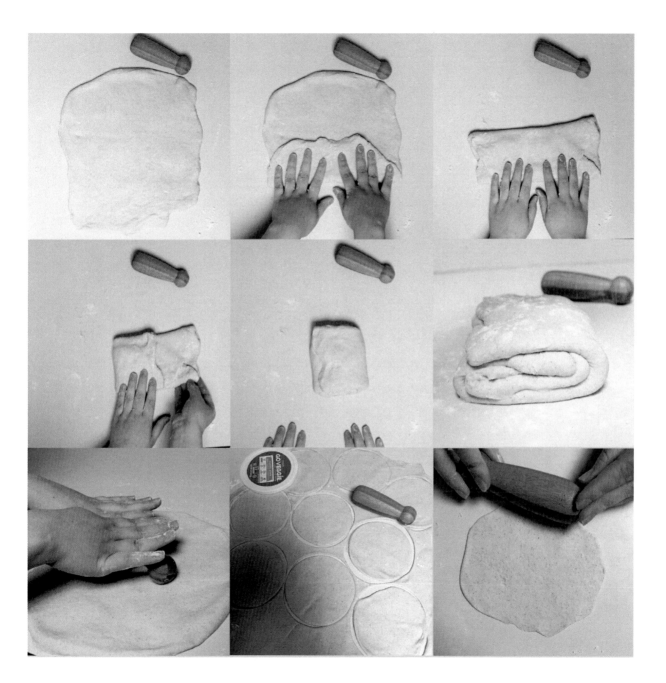

# Pumpkin Empanadas (makes 12)

**DOUGH**
1 ¾ cups (410 ml) flour
¼ tsp (1.25 ml) salt
6 tbsp (90 ml) fat (butter has better flavor but shortening has better texture)
1 tsp (5 ml) vinegar
½ cup (120 ml) cold water
1 tsp cinnamon (5 ml)

**PUMPKIN FILLING**
1 ¾ cups (420 ml) pumpkin purée
¾ cup (180 ml) full fat coconut milk
½ cup (120 ml) sweetener
½ cup (120 ml) starch
1 tsp (5 ml) vanilla extract
2 tsp (10 ml) pumpkin pie spice
½ tsp (2.5 ml) salt
¼ cup (60 ml) ground flaxseeds

**DOUGH**
1. In a large bowl, whisk together flour and salt. Using a pastry cutter or fork, cut in the fat until it has the texture of chunky sand. Avoid using hands as the warmth will begin to melt the fat and that is what gives the crust it's flaky texture.
2. Add cold water and vinegar, stirring with a fork. If the dough is still too dry add a tablespoon at a time and mix.
3. After the batter is well mixed, flour a flat surface and roll the dough out.
4. Fold the left side a third of the way over. Fold the right side a third of the way over. Fold the bottom a third of the way over. Fold the top a third of the way over. Repeat until it forms a cub
5. Roll it out again, adding more flour if needed and repeat 5 times to create layers for a flaky dough.
6. Wrap tightly with plastic wrap and place in a container with a lid. Put it in the refrigerator for 1-2 hours.

Discs can be made one of two ways:
a. Roll all the dough out to a desired thickness-- the sweet spot is 3/16 inches. Place a circular object on top of the dough like a lid and press down, it will cut through the dough. Repeat process with dough scraps.
b. Separate the dough into equal sized spheres. Then, roll them out as circular as possible.
Freeze by stacking each disc on top of one another with parchment paper in between and store in an airtight container.

## FILLING
1. Mix pumpkin, full fat coconut milk, and vanilla in a bowl.
2. Mix in all other ingredients.

## ASSEMBLY
1. Take a spoonful of pumpkin filling and place it in the center of the disc.
2. Fold in half and press the very edge of the circumference down with a fork.
3. Flip over and repeat. They should look like half moons.
4. Poke the top of the empanada with a fork.
5. Brush the top with almond milk.
6. Place on a lined baking tray and bake at 400 degrees for 30 minutes flipping halfway.
7. Serve.

See a diagram for the dough on page 127.

# Coconut Limber (Coconut Icee)

1 ½ cups (350 ml) coconut milk
3 tbsp (45 ml) sweetener

1. Add all ingredients into a sealable jar or popsicle mold. Stir or shake.
2. Taste for sweetness and adjust as needed. When satisfied, top and freeze overnight.
3. Untop the next day and serve.

# Coconut Pineapple Limber (Coconut Pineapple Icee)

¾ cup (180 ml) pineapple juice
¾ cup (180 ml) coconut milk
2 tbsp (30 ml) sweetener

1. Add all ingredients into a sealable jar or popsicle mold. Stir or shake.
2. Taste for sweetness and adjust as needed. When satisfied, freeze overnight.
3. Untop and serve.

# Pineapple Limber (Pineapple Icee)

1 ½ cups (350 ml) pineapple juice
1 tbsp (15 ml) sweetener

1. Add all ingredients into a sealable jar or popsicle mold. Stir or shake.
2. Taste for sweetness and adjust as needed. When satisfied, freeze overnight.
3. Untop and serve.

TIPS:
You can use anything from plastic disposable cups to silicone molds.
Some popular flavors are cherry, lemon, orange, concentrated tamarind, and mango.

# Mantecaditos (Shortbread Cookies)

1 cup (240 ml) flour
¼ cup (60 ml) sugar
½ cup (120 ml) vegan butter
½ tsp (5 ml) vanilla extract
pinch of salt
sprinkles or guava paste on top

1. Cream butter and sugar. Add vanilla and salt to the bowl.
2. Sift in flour and mix until well combined.
3. Using your hands, pull pieces of dough and roll them into balls about 1 inch in diameter.
4. Place them on a lined baking tray.
5. Press a teaspoon or thumb in the center of the dough to create a dip.
6. Cut slices of guava or scoop a spoonful of sprinkles and place it in the middle of each cookie.
7. Bake at 400 degrees for 15 minutes or until the bottoms turn slightly brown.
8. Cool and serve.

If you don't have access to guava or vegan sprinkles, try powdered sugar.

# Guava Cheesecake

**FILLING**
1 ½ cups (350 ml) raw unsalted cashews, soaked
⅓ cup (80 ml) coconut oil
2 tbsp (30 ml) lemon juice
1 tsp (5 ml) vanilla extract
¼ cup (60 ml) sweetener
½ cup (120 ml) full fat coconut milk
½ cup (120 ml) guava paste

**CRUST**
¼ tsp (1.25 ml) cinnamon
14 graham crackers or 2 cups (475 ml) smashed cookies
6 tbsp (90 ml) melted vegan butter

1. After soaking cashews, strain, rinse, and add to a blender.
2. Add remaining ingredients and blend until creamy.
3. Mash graham crackers into fine small crumbs. I used a ziploc bag and pestle.
4. Add crushed crackers, cinnamon, and melted butter into a mold. Mix until well combined.
5. Press it on the bottom of the mold until it forms a solid crust.
6. Pour mixture into pan and set in the freezer for an hour or until firm.
7. Cut and serve.

Feel free to swap graham crackers for another biscuit cookie. You can experiment with the guava. Pour some sauce on top of this plain cheesecake or swirl guava paste into the cake before setting into the freezer.

# DIMITRI'S RECIPES

My partner, Dimitri, is a lot more open to food than I am. He loves maduros and mushrooms and adds his own sabor when he decides to enter the kitchen.

# Tostones Rellenos (Stuffed Plantain Cups)
## w/ Garbanzo Bean Stew

**PLANTAIN CUPS**
3 unripe plantains
oil
salt, veggie broth (optional)

**GARBANZO BEAN STEW FILLING**
1 ½ cups (350 ml) garbanzo beans
½ cup (120 ml) water
1 ½ tbsp (22.5 ml) sofrito
2 ½ tbsp (37.5 ml) tomato sauce
½ tsp (2.5 ml) adobo
½ tsp (2.5 ml) sazón

1.  Set water to boil in a medium pot.
2.  Cut off the ends of the plantains and slit the peels lengthwise. Make sure to only slice the depth of the skin.
3.  Take a knife and hold the plantain firmly with the sliced side facing you. Wedge the knife between the slice   and move the knife to the left and right. This helps to remove the skin from the plantain. Do this from one side of the plantain to the other.
4.  After putting your knife down, slide your thumbs under the skin until you've removed it from the plantain.
5.  Chop them into fourths and set them to boil for 20 minutes in plain water, salted water, or vegetable broth.
6.  Oil a muffin tin (I used a 12 count.)
7.  When the plantains are fork tender, evenly place plantains into each of the 12 sections.
8.  Take a pestle and mash, until a plantain cup is created. Mold the plantain in the tin where necessary.
9.  Set it to bake in the oven at 400 degrees for 40 minutes or until the plantain cups are crispy.
10. While the cups are baking in the oven, heat oil in a pan and add sofrito.
11. After 30 seconds add adobo, sazón, tomato sauce, water, and beans.
12. Cook until most of the sauce is gone, alternatively add chopped spinach to sop up sauce and add extra nutrients.
13. Additionally, you can make the guacamole recipe to put on top.
14. Once plantain cups are cooked use a butter knife to pull the cups away from the tin. Gently remove them, being sure to not rip the bottom.
15. Place the plantain cups on a plate and fill with ingredients. Serve.

# Maduros ("Fried" Sweet Plantains)

2 yellow or black plantains
1 tbsp (15 ml) oil

1. Ripened plantains are softer and easier to prepare than green plantains.
2. After the ends are cut, slit the peels lengthwise. Make sure to only slice the depth of the skin.
3. Take a knife and hold the plantain firmly with the sliced side facing you. Wedge the knife between the slice and move the knife to the left and right. This helps to remove the skin from the plantain. Do this from one side of the plantain to the other.
4. After putting your knife down, slide your thumbs under the skin until you've removed it from the plantain.
5. Peel and slice plantains ½ inch thick.
6. Add to a bowl with oil and spices.
7. Place on a lined baking tray and cook at 400 degrees for 30 minutes. Flip them halfway.
8. Serve.

BE CAREFUL when cutting the plantains and removing the skin.

Sweet plantains are very slippery!

# Pastelon (Sweet Plantain Lasagna)

**PLANTAIN**
1 tbsp (15 ml) oil
3 yellow or black plantains

**MUSHROOM PICADILLO ("MUSHROOM HASH")**
1 tsp (5 ml) oil
¾ cup (180 ml) minced green and red peppers
½ cup (120 ml) minced onion
3 cups (700 ml) minced mushroom
1 ½ cups (350 ml) tomato sauce
¼ cup (60 ml) sofrito
1 tsp (5 ml) adobo
1 tsp (5 ml) sazón
¼ tsp (1.25 ml) black pepper
spinach (optional)

**BINDING SAUCE**
1 tsp (5 ml) vegan butter
⅓ cup (80 ml) plant milk
¼ tsp (1.25 ml) turmeric
1 tsp (5 ml) starch

I strongly encourage some vegan cheese for this meal as cheese is traditionally used. The binding sauce I've created is only for binding and not flavor.

1. Ripened plantains are softer and easier to prepare than green plantains. BE CAREFUL when cutting off the ends of the plantains. They're soft and slippery.
2. After the ends are cut, slit the peels lengthwise. Make sure to only slice the depth of the skin.
3. Take a knife and hold the plantain firmly with the sliced side facing you. Wedge the knife between the slice and move the knife to the left and right. This helps to remove the skin from the plantain. Do this from one side of the plantain to the other.
4. After putting your knife down, slide your thumbs under the skin until you've removed it from the plantain.
5. Cut plantain in half, then cut the halves into ¼ inch slices. Mix plantain with oil and optional spices.
6. Place on a lined baking tray and bake at 400 degrees for 20 minutes. Flip halfway.
7. While in the oven, begin to prepare the mushroom picadillo.
8. Finely mince garlic, onion, and peppers. Add them to a greased pan, sauteing until caramelized.
9. Finely dice a package of mushrooms or chop in a food processor. Place in the pan to saute until they reach a desired browning.
10. Add in sofrito, adobo, sazón, and tomato sauce, heating through to make sure you get the mixture mostly dried out. A wet mixture will cause your dish to be runny. Add spinach if too liquidy.
11. If not using Vegan cheese, prepare the binding sauce by melting butter in a pan and adding milk, spices, and sifting in starch. Stir until thick.
12. Pull plantain out of the oven and begin assembling like a lasagna. Lay flat the plantain slices, then sauce, then mushroom picadillo, and repeat until you run out. Make sure to add a bit more sauce to the top layer.
13. Bake at 400 degrees for 20 minutes or until crispy. Serve.

# Canoas (Sweet Plantain Canoes)

**PLATANO CANOAS**
3 ripened plantains
oil to coat

**MUSHROOM PICADILLO ("MUSHROOM HASH")**
1 tsp (5 ml) oil
¾ cup (180 ml) minced green and red peppers
½ cup (120 ml) minced onion
3 cups (700 ml) minced mushroom
1 ½ cups (350 ml) tomato sauce
¼ cup (60 ml) sofrito
1 tsp (5 ml) adobo
1 tsp (5 ml) sazón
¼ tsp (1.25 ml) black pepper
spinach (optional)

**BINDING SAUCE**
1 tsp (5 ml) vegan butter
⅓ cup (80 ml) plant milk
¼ tsp (1.25 ml) turmeric
1 tsp (5 ml) starch

For a faster meal, use tvp picadillo instead.

1. Ripened plantains are softer and easier to prepare than green plantains. BE CAREFUL when cutting off the ends of the plantains. They're soft and slippery.
2. Cut off the ends of the plantains and slit the peels lengthwise. Make sure to only slice the depth of the skin.
3. Take a knife and hold the plantain firmly with the sliced side facing you. Wedge the knife between the slice and move the knife to the left and right. This helps to remove the skin from the plantain. Do this from one side of the plantain to the other.
4. After putting your knife down, slide your thumbs under the skin until you've removed it from the plantain.
5. Rub the entire plantain with oil and place it on a lined baking tray for 20 minutes flip over and bake for another 15 minutes.
6. While plantains are in the oven, begin to prepare the mushroom picadillo.
7. Finely mince garlic, onion, and peppers. Add them to a greased pan, sauteing until caramelized.
8. Finely dice a package of mushrooms or chop in a food processor. Place in the pan to saute until they reach a desired browning.
9. Add in sofrito, adobo, sazón, and tomato sauce, heating through to make sure you get the mixture mostly dried out. A wet mixture will cause your dish to be runny. Add spinach if too liquidy.
10. If not using Vegan cheese, prepare the sauce by melting butter in a pan and adding milk, spices, and sifting in starch. Stir until thick.
11. Take the plantain out of the oven and slice it down the middle, being sure not to cut it all the way though. Slices should be 1 cm away from both ends of the plantain.
12. Lay plantain with the opening facing up like a canoe. Fill with mushroom picadillo and sauce.
13. Bake at 400 for 10- 15 minutes. Serve.

# Albondigas ("Meatballs") (Lentilballs)

**LENTILBALLS**
2 cups (480 ml) boiled lentils in vegetable broth
½ cup (120 ml) minced onion
⅓ cup (80 ml) minced green pepper
⅓ cup (80 ml) minced red pepper
1 tsp (5 ml) adobo
1 tsp (5 ml) sazón
½ bunch minced cilantro
1 minced garlic clove
flour of choice (optional)

**PUERTO RICAN PASTA SAUCE**
1 tsp (5 ml) oil
1 bayleaf
3 tbsp (45 ml) sofrito
1 cup (240 ml) tomato sauce
½ cup (120 ml) water
⅓ cup (80 ml) green and red peppers
½ cup (120 ml) chopped onion
1 tsp (5 ml) adobo
1 tsp (5 ml) sazón
1 sliced carrot

1. Boil lentils in vegetable broth until soft.
2. Oil a pan and caramelize onions and garlic. Then add peppers and caramelize.
3. Roughly mash lentils before adding to the same oiled pan with adobo and sazón.
4. Get the mixture dry enough to form into balls.
5. Mix flour and cilantro.
6. Once cooled enough to handle, form into balls with oil and place on a lined baking tray.
7. Bake at 400 degrees for 30-40 minutes. Flip halfway.
8. While the albondigas are in the oven, work on the pasta sauce.
9. In an oiled pan, caramelize onion and peppers. Then add sliced carrots.
10. Add sofrito, adobo, sazón, and bayleaf.
11. Add tomato sauce and water. Boil with lid on until carrots are soft.
12. Take lentil balls out of the oven and add them to the sauce. Serve.

# Pimientos Rellenos (Stuffed Peppers)

PEPPERS
3 medium sized peppers
½ - 1 tsp (2.5- 5 ml) oil
salt, garlic, onion to taste

LENTIL PICADILLO (LENTIL HASH OR MINCE)
1 tsp (5 ml) oil
¼ tsp (1.25 ml) ground cumin
½ tsp (2.5 ml) salt
1 ½ cups (350 ml) water
4 ½ tbsp (67.5 ml) sofrito
½ cup (120 ml) tomato sauce
1 ½ tsp (7.5 ml) adobo
1 ½ tsp (7.5 ml) sazón
1 ⅛ cups (270 ml) dried lentils soaked 30 minutes boiled
1 medium potato
chopped spinach

1. Set lentils to boil.
2. Cube potatoes. When the lentils begin to boil, throw the potato in.
3. While lentils are boiling, slice the tops off of the peppers and remove the cores. Make sure to wash out any remaining seeds and to not discard the tops. They're needed for later.
4. The lentils and potatoes are done when they are fork tender.
5. In an oiled pan, add sofrito and cook through. Then add adobo, sazón, and tomato sauce. When tomato sauce has heated through, add the lentil/ potato mixture.
6. While the filling is being cooked, grease the insides of the peppers and the bottom of the caps by spreading the oil with your fingers or a brush. Sprinkle salt, onion powder, and garlic powder as desired.
7. Cook until sauce is thick and most of the liquid is absorbed. A saucier filling will be too runny.
8. Evenly scoop lentil picadillo into the peppers, put the caps back on, and carefully place them on a lined baking tray.
9. Bake the peppers at 400 degrees for 20 minutes or until the caps begin to crisp.

# Guineo en Escabeche (Pickled Green Banana Salad)

6 green bananas
6 tbsp (90 ml) plant milk
½ onion sliced
3 tbsp (45 ml) vinegar
½ cup (120 ml) oil
3 minced garlic cloves
½ minced red pepper
½ minced green pepper
2 bay leaves
¾ tsp (3.75 ml) salt
¾ tsp (3.75 ml) black pepper
½ tsp (2.5 ml) garlic powder
½ tsp (2.5 ml) onion powder
¼ tsp (1.25 ml) turmeric

1. Set water to boil in a large pot with milk.
2. Oil your hands and cut off the ends of the bananas. Slitting the peels lengthwise. Make sure to only slice the depth of the skin. Then cut the bananas in half.
3. Add to boiling water for 20- 25 minutes
4. While bananas are boiling, slice and mince all remaining ingredients accordingly.
5. Combine onions and vinegar in a bowl to marinade.
6. Add oil, red pepper, green pepper, garlic cloves, bay leaves and spices to a different pot and heat on medium for 7 minutes. Then stir in the vinegar and onions.
7. Put the lid on for an additional 7 minutes. Do not fry.
8. In the meantime, strain the bananas and use tongs or a fork to take the peels off.
9. After they've cooled, slice them into ½ inch discs and add them to a wide container. This will allow them to be evenly soaked in the marinade.
10. Add oil and vinegar mixture into the container. If you wanted to add extra spices, now would be the appropriate time.
11. Put a lid on and marinade it for several hours. The flavor gets stronger the longer you leave it.

# Berenjenas Guisadas (Eggplant Stew)

2 tbsp (30 ml) oil
3 minced garlic cloves
¾ cup (180 ml) chopped onion
½ cup (120 ml) cubed green pepper
½ cup (120 ml) cubed red pepper
4 tbsp (60 ml) sofrito
¾ cup (180 ml) tomato sauce
½ tsp (2.5 ml) oregano
¼ tsp (1.25 ml) ground cumin
1 tsp (5 ml) sazón
1 tsp (5 ml) adobo
½ tsp (2.5 ml) salt
¼ tsp (1.25 ml) black pepper
2 lbs (910 g) cubed eggplant
handful of chopped spinach

1. Chop all ingredients. Add oil to a pan and heat through.
2. Add garlic for 30 seconds. Add onions and caramelize.
3. Add green and red peppers. Caramelize.
4. Add sofrito and heat through.
5. Stir in tomato sauce and spices.
6. Add eggplant, mix, and top for 10 minutes.
7. Stir and add the lid again for 7 minutes.
8. Add spinach, turn off the burner, and leave topped for 3 minutes or until desired texture. Serve.

This recipe can also be used as a dip.

[Puerto Rican Vegan Cookbook] 157

# Quesitos (Cream Cheese Turnovers)

**FILLING**
8 oz (225 g) vegan cream cheese
3 tbsp (45 ml) sugar
1 tsp (5 ml) vanilla extract

**PASTRY**
1 cup (240 ml) + 2 tbsp (30 ml) flour
¼ tsp (1.25 ml) salt
5 tbsp (75 ml) cold water
¼ cup (60 ml) vegan butter
(tip: diagram for pastry on page 127

sugar for sprinkling
milk for browning
agave for glazing

1. Scoop butter into a bowl. Sift in flour and salt. Fork until well combined.
2. Add cold water and mix. You can use your hands but I prefer a silicone spatula. Mixing with your hand can melt the butter and the cold fat helps the cough maintain flakiness.
3. After the batter is well mixed, flour a flat surface and roll the dough out.
4. Fold the left side a third of the way over. Fold the right side a third of the way over. Fold the bottom a third of the way over. Fold the top a third of the way over. Repeat until it forms a cube.
5. Roll it out again, adding more flour if needed and repeat 5 times to create layers for a flaky dough.
6. Wrap tightly with plastic wrap and place in a container with a lid. Put it in the refrigerator for 1-2 hours.
7. In a bowl, scoop out the entire Vegan cream cheese container. Mix in vanilla extract and sugar.
8. When the dough is ready, flour a flat surface and roll back out until it forms a square and cut into 9 even quadrants.
9. Place a square of dough onto a lined baking sheet diagonally, so that it looks like a diamond shape. Scoop in one tablespoon of Vegan cream cheese mix into the center.
10. Fold one corner over the cream cheese, then the other corner on top of that corner and repeat.
11. After all 9 are on the tray. Brush plant milk onto the top and sprinkle sugar.
12. Bake at 400 degrees for 18 minutes or until lightly browned.
13. Take them out and glaze them with agave or other sweetener. Serve.

# Baked Barriguitas de Vieja (Pumpkin Fritter)

1 ½ cup (300 ml) pumpkin

½ cup (120 ml) sugar

1 tsp (5 ml) vanilla extract

1 tbsp (15 ml) flax meal

2 tbsp (30 ml) baking powder

½ cup (120 ml) flour

¼ tsp (1.25 ml) salt

1 tsp (5 ml) cinnamon

½ cup (120 ml) powdered sugar (as topping)

1. Mix all ingredients into a bowl, adding the flour in last.
2. The consistency should look like batter; viscous enough to make dollops with a spoon.
3. Heat up enough oil on a pan to submerge the Barriguitas. Flip them halfway through frying.
4. Before serving, sprinkle them with powdered sugar.

No matter how many times I tried baking this recipe, my Barriguitas would not get crispy. My suggestion would be frying them on the stove or in an air fryer.

# Honorable Mentions

Still feeling adventurous? Here are some recipes that didn't make it into the book.

Bacalaitos (Cod Fish Fritter)
Pernil (Pork Shoulder)
Arroz con Salchichas (Rice and Vienna Sausage)
Mofongo (Fried Mashed Plantain Ball)
Alcapurrias (Root Vegetable Fritters)
Bistec (Steak)
Corned Beef and Fries
Sandwiches de Mezcla (Sandwich Mix)
Sopa de Salchichon (Salami Soup)
Bacalao (Cod Fish Stew)
Pinchos (Kabobs)
Chuleta (Pork Chop)
Rellenos de Papa (Stuffed Potato Balls)
Piononos (Fried Stuffed Ripe Plantains)
Sweet Plantain Empanadas
Papa Rellenas (Stuffed Potatoes)
Mallorcas (Ham and Egg Sandwich)
Arepas o Dumplines o Tortas (Fried Dough)
Arañitas (Little Spiders- Shredded Fried Plantain)
Casabe (Cassava Bread)

Flan
Meringues
Tornillos de Crema (Cream Screw- Pastry)
Tieritas (Planter Pot Desserts)
Tres Leches (Three Milks Cake)
Bolitas de Tamarino (Tamarind Balls)
Ponque (Puerto Rican Pound Cake)
Coquito (Puerto Rican Eggnog)
Horchata de Arroz (Rice Drink)

THERE'S A SHOCKING FACT FLOATING AROUND THE INTERNET THAT SAYS PEOPLE
ONLY MAKE 3-5 RECIPES FROM COOKBOOKS. I ENCOURAGE YOU TO MAKE MORE THAN THAT.
PLAY AROUND IN THE KITCHEN, HAVE FUN, AND TAKE PRIDE.

You can tag me on Instagram @ MinimaistVeganLifestyle or my partner @Dimitri__Reyes

Mucho Sabor y Amor